1

Civil Defense and Homeland Security: A Short History of National Preparedness Efforts

Introduction

From the air raid warning and plane spotting activities of the Office of Civil Defense in the 1940s, to the *Duck and Cover* film strips and backyard shelters of the 1950s, to today's all-hazards preparedness programs led by the Department of Homeland Security, Federal strategies to enhance the nation's preparedness for disaster and attack have evolved over the course of the 20th century and into the 21st.

Presidential administrations can have a powerful impact on both national and citizen preparedness. By recommending funding levels, creating new policies, and implementing new programs; successive administrations have adapted preparedness efforts to align with changing domestic priorities and foreign policy goals. They have also instituted administrative reorganizations that reflected their preference for consolidated or dispersed civil defense and homeland security responsibilities within the Federal government.

Programs were seldom able to get ahead of world events, and were ultimately challenged in their ability to answer the public's need for protection from threats due to bureaucratic turbulence created by frequent reorganization, shifting funding priorities, and varying levels of support by senior policymakers. This in turn has had an effect on the public's perception of national preparedness. Public awareness and support have waxed and waned over the years, as the government's emphasis on national preparedness has shifted.

An analysis of the history of civil defense and homeland security programs in the United States clearly indicates that to be considered successful, national preparedness programs must be long in their reach yet cost effective. They must also be appropriately tailored to the Nation's diverse communities, be carefully planned, capable of quickly providing pertinent information to the populace about imminent threats, and able to convey risk without creating unnecessary alarm.

The following narrative identifies some of the key trends, drivers of change, and lessons learned in the history of U.S. national preparedness programs. A review of the history of these programs will assist the Federal government in its efforts to develop and implement effective homeland security policy and better understand previous national preparedness initiatives.

Pre-Cold War Period (1917-1945)

World War I introduced a new type of attack: the use of strategic aerial strikes against an enemy's population to degrade its ability and will to wage war. German aerial bombardment of towns in countries such as France, Belgium, and Poland began in August 1914, and in the following year Kaiser Wilhelm authorized sustained bombing campaigns against military and civilian targets, particularly against England.[1] From May through October of 1915, Germany launched seven air strikes against London alone.[2] England, like most other nations at the time, did not have an organized civil defense program to aid citizens during such attacks. Individuals were forced to find their own way to safety, often taking refuge in the city's underground subway stations.[3] By all assessments, the damage and casualty figures that resulted from these early bombing operations were comparatively insignificant, but they exerted a psychological toll on the British public.[4] It became clear that civilian defense, involving a range of actions to protect the general public in the event of attack, would become a major fixture in future warfare.

Though the Axis and Allied powers continued to employ strategic bombing throughout World War I, leaders in the United States did not feel that the country was vulnerable to attack. They concentrated their public outreach on rallying support for the war effort.[5] Much of this task was coordinated by the **Council of National Defense**, established on August 29, 1916 with the passage of an Army appropriations bill.[6] The Council was a presidential advisory board that included the Secretaries of War, Navy, Interior, Agriculture, Commerce, and Labor; assisted by an Advisory Committee appointed by the President.[7] Its responsibilities included "coordinating resources and industries for national defense" and "stimulating civilian morale."[8]

The work of the Council escalated when the United States entered the war in 1917. In the same year, the Federal government asked State governors to create their own local councils of defense to support the National effort.[9] However, the Council's activities continued to focus more on facilitating mobilization for the war than on protecting civilian resources. When hostilities ended, the Council shifted its efforts toward demobilization. Its operations were suspended in June, 1921.[10]

For the remainder of the 1920s, the Federal government undertook little public outreach related to defense and security. However, the 1930s saw a revival of civil defense efforts, when aggressive actions and arms stockpiling in Europe fueled international concern.[11] In 1933, President Franklin Roosevelt created by executive order the **National Emergency Council** (NEC) which consisted of the President, his Cabinet members, and the head of nearly every major Federal agency, commission, and board.[12] The mission of the NEC included a variety of programs unrelated to civil defense; however, its duties also included coordination of emergency programs among all agencies involved in national preparedness.[13]

As World War II ignited in Europe, Roosevelt reestablished the Council of National Defense in 1940.[14] Once again States were asked to establish local counterpart councils. Tensions among Federal, State and local governments began to rise about authority and resources.

The states claimed they were not given enough power to manage civil defense tasks in their own jurisdictions, and local governments asserted that State governments did not give urban areas proper consideration and resources.[15] Non-attack disaster preparedness remained almost entirely the responsibility of States, while federal funding was reserved primarily for attack preparedness.

Because of extensive civilian bombing campaigns in Europe, concerns about possible attacks against the U.S. homeland increased. Mayor Fiorello La Guardia of New York City wrote a letter to President Roosevelt stating:

> "There is a need for a strong Federal Department to coordinate activities, and not only to coordinate but to initiate and get things going. Please bear in mind that up to this war and never in our history, has the civilian population been exposed to attack. The new technique of war has created the necessity for developing new techniques of civilian defense".[16]

President Roosevelt responded to the increasing concern of the public and local officials by creating the **Office of Civilian Defense** (OCD) in 1941.[17] The President delegated a number of responsibilities to the OCD by broadly interpreting civilian protection to include morale maintenance, promotion of volunteer involvement, and nutrition and physical education.[18] The OCD oversaw unprecedented federal involvement in attack preparedness. As with the Council of National Defense, the OCD created corresponding defense councils at the local level.[19]

The issue of whether the OCD should emphasize protective services, typically done at that time by men, or social welfare services, typically undertaken at that time by women, created tension from the office's inception.[20] Director Fiorello LaGuardia referred to "nonprotective" activities as "sissy stuff" and saw opportunities to build neighborhood militias. Pressured to focus on other nonprotective areas such as neighborhood support, he appointed Eleanor Roosevelt to expand volunteer activities.[21] The two leaders, with their radically divergent points of view, exemplified a conflict over the meaning and purpose of civil defense that would continue well into the cold war era.

OCD received criticism from Congress and the public on several fronts. It was called "pink" by influential politicians who disliked the program's broad reach and social development programs. Some believed the organization's tasks were better undertaken by the Department of War.[22] One of OCD's early leaders, James Landis, recommended that the organization be abolished, since the threat of an attack on U.S. civilians had receded.[23]

With the end of World War II, most U.S. officials agreed that the risk of an attack on the U.S. homeland was minimal. Roosevelt did not take Landis' suggestion, and the OCD continued to operate.[24] While the OCD did not fulfill all of its ambitious goals, it did begin the development of concrete civil defense plans, including air raid drills, black outs, and sand bag stockpiling.[25]

Truman Administration (1945-1953)

Soon after taking office, Harry Truman did follow Landis' advice and abolished the OCD, reflecting the widely held belief that the immediate threat of war had receded. [26] Initially, civil defense was not a high priority in the Truman Administration, as troops began to return home and other war time offices were diminished in scale or disbanded altogether. The development of the atomic bomb, however, had opened up previously unthinkable risks. Increasing hostilities with the Soviet Union and their pursuit of a nuclear bomb threatened the United States.

In this context, Truman began to reexamine the national defense structure, reviewing the results of a set of commissions.[27] In 1946, the U.S. Strategic Bombing Survey published its report evaluating the results of strategic bombing campaigns by imperial Germany and Japan against enemy civilian populations. The report indicated that civil defense plans could significantly mitigate the effects of strategic bombing.[28] Specifically, mass evacuation plans for urban areas and shelters for those unable to leave the area could form components of a viable civil defense plan.[29] In 1947, the War Department's Civil Defense Board, led by Major General Harold Bull, released a second report.[30] The so-called *Bull Report* stated that civil defense is the responsibility of civilians, and the military should not be expected to get involved in such matters.[31] According to the report, civil defense was best implemented locally, a concept referred to as "self-help". Still, the document did concede that the Federal government could provide the majority of necessary resources.[32] Additionally, Congress passed the National Security Act of 1947. Best known for the creation of the Central Intelligence Agency, the Act also created the **National Security Resources Board** (NSRB), which was initially responsible for mobilizing civilian and military support, as well as maintaining adequate reserves and effective resource use in the event of war.[33]

Neither report resulted in substantial reforms to the Truman Administration's policies because civil defense continued to remain a low priority.[34] However, as U.S.-Soviet relations became increasingly strained, President Truman began to implement civil defense policy reforms. These changes resulted, in part, from the strong recommendation of Colonel Burnet Beers, who was responsible for directing a study on future civil defense planning and operations to establish a civil defense unit in the Office of the Secretary of Defense (OSD).[35] Truman acted promptly on this advice, establishing the **Office of Civil Defense Planning** (OCDP), whose purpose was to recommend a course for the creation of a permanent civil defense agency.[36] After six months, the OCDP released its 300-page *Hopley Report*,[37] which called for the creation of a Federal office of civil defense directly under the President or Secretary of Defense. The report additionally recommended that the Federal government provide civil defense guidance and assistance, but that State and local governments handle most of the operational responsibilities.[38]

Reactions to the *Hopley Report* inside and outside government were generally negative. There were concerns about the cost and scope of civil defense. Many people feared its recommendations were too far-reaching and made unrealistic demands on the public and government.[39] And there were concerns about military control. Some civilian groups thought the report called for transferring what should be a civilian responsibility to the military, which could lead to a "garrison state."[40]

Truman ultimately chose to address the latter concern by assigning civil defense planning to the NSRB, a civilian agency.[41] However, the NSRB did not receive the necessary resources or authority to carry out its mandate.[42] As a result, the Board was moved to the Department of Defense (DOD), then shifted to the Executive Office of the President, and finally had its responsibilities transferred to the **Office of Defense Mobilization** in December of 1950.

The climate of civil defense changed dramatically with the successful Soviet test of a nuclear weapon in August of 1949. The United States lost its monopoly on nuclear weapons and the corresponding negotiating power that this entailed. Local officials began to demand from the Federal government a clear outline of what they were to do in crisis situations.[43] The Truman Administration received criticism from local officials, a worried American public, and Congress for not taking firm action.[44] In response, in 1950, the NSRB generated a new proposal called the *Blue Book*, which outlined a set of civil defense functions and how they should be implemented at each level of government.[45] The *Blue Book* also recommended the creation of an independent Federal civil defense organization.[46]

Truman agreed with many of the *Blue Book* recommendations, but held firm to his belief that civil defense responsibilities should fall mostly on the shoulders of the State and local governments.[47] In response, Congress enacted the Federal Civil Defense Act of 1950, which placed most of the civil defense burden on the States and created the **Federal Civil Defense Administration** (FCDA) to formulate national policy to guide the States' efforts.[48]

As planning began, policymakers struggled to define what was meant by national security. A key question was the appropriate level of readiness to be attained. At what readiness level would people have to surrender personal freedoms to state control? At what level of security would civil defense metamorphose into a garrison state, undermining the underlying purpose of protecting individual rights?[49] The decision to assign civil defense responsibility to States and localities was intended partly as a safeguard against the garrison state.

Planners also struggled with a difficult political question: just how much support should government provide? Congressional resistance to paying for a comprehensive program, and concerns about establishing public dependency on government, led to adoption of a doctrine of "self help": individual responsibility for preparedness to minimize (not eliminate) risk.[50] The idea of decentralized, locally controlled, volunteer-based civil defense was not new; in fact it was the foundation of the successful British civil defense effort in World War II. However, the decision to make self-help the basis of civil defense was also a political compromise, a way to balance conflicting views over the size, power, and priorities of the emerging postwar nation.[51]

The FCDA led shelter building programs, sought to improve Federal and State coordination, established an attack warning system, stockpiled supplies, and started a well known national civic education campaign. In 1952, the FCDA joined with the Ad Council to release Korean War advertising to boost national morale.[52] The FCDA specifically aimed to teach schoolchildren about preparedness, primarily through civil defense drills.[53] In order to effectively educate the entire youth population, the FCDA commissioned a movie studio to produce nine civil defense movies that would be shown in classrooms across the nation – among them *Duck and Cover*.[54] The movie, through its main character Bert the Turtle, showed children what to do when they saw "the flash of an atomic bomb."[55] Newspapers and experts generally heralded the film as a positive and optimistic step toward preparedness.[56] The *New York Herald Tribune*, for example, called the film "very instructive" and "not too frightening for children."[57] Ultimately, the

film was seen by millions of schoolchildren during the 1950s.[58] The public education campaign throughout the decade promoted the idea that with preparation, a nuclear attack could be survivable.[59]

Photo Removed Due to Copyright Restrictions

Duck and Cover promotional material

An examination of the FCDA-led shelter-building initiative underscores some of the civil defense program's internal inconsistencies. The Federal Civil Defense Act of 1950 allocated significant funding to a shelter initiative. The law allowed the FCDA to develop shelter designs and make financial contributions to shelter programs. However, Congress stipulated that the Federal government could not finance the construction of new shelters.[60] In communities across the country there was great debate over the necessity of the shelters, and Truman himself was not eager to spend government money on the program.[61] Moreover, FCDA Administrator Millard Caldwell initiated a public relations fiasco when he misconstrued the shelter program as a means to protect every person in the country. A program that expansive was deemed to be too costly to receive sufficient political support; as a result, it never left the planning stages during the Truman Administration.[62]

Contrary to the outlook offered by *Duck and Cover* and the other educational campaigns, early media reports about the possibility of nuclear war offered grim predictions concerning the aftermath of an attack. The scenarios were horrific, and the association of civil defense with death and destruction made not only home preparedness and sheltering, but the whole self-help preparedness concept, a tough sell.[63]

The political, fiscal, and emotional cross-currents were reflected in civil defense funding. Despite ambitious funding requests, actual appropriations to civil defense remained low throughout the Truman Administration, and throughout the 1950s. For example, from 1951 to 1953 Truman requested $1.5 billion for civil defense, but appropriations totaled only $153 million – 90 percent less than requested[64].

Despite these practical setbacks, the concept of civil defense as a purposeful approach to the protection of citizens from threats outside the Nation's borders began to take shape during Truman's presidency.[65] Though each leader who followed would focus on different programs and approaches, civil defense remained an important initiative during the coming decades.

Eisenhower Administration (1953-1961)

President Dwight Eisenhower's approach to civil defense was quite different from his predecessor's. Eisenhower identified the enormous economic commitment required for military development as one reason not to undertake expensive civil defense programs.[66] Additionally, Republicans in Congress were eager to curtail spending, as the party had publicly promised to balance the budget when Eisenhower took office.[67] Though Eisenhower requested less funding than Truman, actual appropriations were virtually identical to appropriations under Truman.[68]

In addition to economic concerns, world events contributed to Eisenhower's decision to support a mass evacuation policy, instead of the shelter program initiated under Truman. In 1953, the Soviets detonated a hydrogen nuclear bomb; and shortly thereafter, the effects of the initial U.S. hydrogen explosion were released to the American public.[69] The blast and thermal effects of these new fusion nuclear weapons were so destructive that many experts argued that American cities would be doomed in the event of a nuclear attack, regardless of sheltering efforts.[70] As a result, new FCDA Administrator Frederick Peterson urged Congress to scale back or completely eliminate the shelter program.[71]

In strongly supporting mass evacuation, Peterson noted that successful execution would depend on sufficient warning time, proper training for civil defense officials, and regular public drills.[72] Many of the responsibilities for evacuation would be borne at the State and local level, which appealed to Eisenhower's belief that the Federal government should not shoulder the entire burden for civil defense programs.[73] Congress also was in favor of the shift in attention from shelters to evacuation.[74] Yet some members, especially Congressman Chet Holifield of California, were adamantly opposed to reducing the shelter system.[75] Holifield was the ranking member of the Joint Committee on Atomic Energy and later the chairman of the Military Operations Subcommittee.[76] In support of a federally funded shelter system, he likened the idea of family built shelters to creating "an army or a navy or an air force by advising each one to buy himself a jet plane."[77] As a well publicized champion for shelter building, Congressman Holifield consistently and persuasively articulated the benefits of shelter building to the American public.

In March of 1954, the United States detonated another thermonuclear bomb, called *Bravo*, on Bikini Atoll in the Marshall Islands.[78] Due to a major wind shift, a large amount of

The 1954 *Bravo* test

radioactive fallout was unexpectedly released over a 7000 square mile area, ultimately poisoning the crew of a Japanese fishing boat in the area and even injuring personnel involved in the test.[79] It did not take long for Congress and the public to turn their attention to the need for shelters to protect the citizenry from such lethal effects.[80] The FCDA was in a tough position. They had just fought for evacuation policies, at the expense of the shelter option, and the Eisenhower Administration continued to support evacuation as the chief civil defense objective.[81] Faced with this dilemma, FCDA Administrator Peterson redirected his policy toward an "evacuation to shelter" approach, whereby individuals would be evacuated from affected areas to shelters.[82] He even proposed digging ditches along roadsides for those who could not get to shelters in time.[83]

The Eisenhower Administration had just begun work on its massive federal highway program, connecting major cities and in the process providing a means for evacuation.[84] Peterson clashed with the President on the program, arguing that Congress should divert some of the highway funding to support civil defense programs. He believed that the highways should be designed to lead only 30 to 40 miles outside of major cities to rural "reception areas."[85] However, Peterson's clout did not match the President's, and thus no money was diverted from the highway program.[86]

The FCDA received extensive criticism over the next few years for not developing a feasible plan for evacuating major cities.[87] Congressman Holifield called FCDA efforts only a façade of civil defense programs.[88] He also chastised the President for not taking more responsibility.[89] At Holifield's request, in 1956 the House Committee on Government Operations held a series of hearings to discuss the viability of the FCDA.[90] The "Holifield Hearings" constituted the largest examination of the civil defense program in U.S. history.[91]

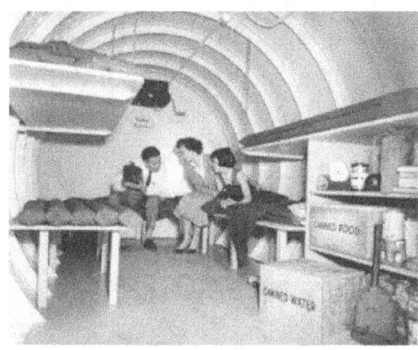

Long Island shelter, circa 1955

Holifield and his Committee concluded that the FCDA had been myopically focused on evacuation, which they termed "a cheap substitute for atomic shelter."[92] The FCDA responded by presenting a National Shelter Policy, which proposed a $32 billion program for "federally subsidized self-help" (e.g. tax incentives or special mortgage rates to shelter-owning families).[93] Taken aback by the cost of the proposal, Eisenhower convened the Gaither Committee (named for its first chairman, H. Rowan Gaither) composed of leading scientific, military, and business experts. The committee evaluated military readiness and concluded that the United States could not defend itself from a Soviet surprise attack on the homeland.[94] While its report, released in 1957, emphasized funding anti-ballistic missile (ABM) defense systems, it also acknowledged that a fallout shelter system occupied a secondary position in deterrence, and to that end recommended adopting the FCDA shelter proposal.[95] Two subsequent reports advanced similar ideas.[96] In 1958, the *Rockefeller Report*, compiled by a board of experts and practitioners directed by Henry Kissinger, stated that civil defense was one aspect of a robust deterrent that should also include more investment in offensive military capabilities.[97] That same year, a report published by the RAND Corporation emphasized the importance of civil defense as a powerful component of deterrence.[98]

Despite these supporting reports, the FCDA shelter proposal continued to run counter to the views of top officials in the Eisenhower Administration. Secretary of State John Foster Dulles argued that the nation should focus resources on retaliation capabilities and curtail the shelter program.[99] Military leaders also opposed the shelter program, fearing it would cut into defense spending.[100] Eisenhower himself remained opposed to the massive shelter program.[101] Instead of pursuing the National Shelter Policy, he instructed the FCDA to initiate much more limited actions, including research on fallout shelters, a survey of existing structures, and informing the public about shelters.[102]

Holifield and other legislators were outraged that the President would disregard the findings of three separate committees.[103] Supporters of the shelter system publicly expressed disappointment with the Eisenhower administration, and Holifield commented that civil defense was in a "deplorable" state during this period.[104] Finally, in the face of strong criticism, Eisenhower largely dissolved the FCDA to make way for the short-lived **Office of Civil and Defense Mobilization** (OCDM), which began the bulk of its work during the Kennedy presidency.[105]

It bears noting that for all of his public opposition to massive sheltering programs, in the middle of his tenure Eisenhower secretly commissioned the building of an underground bunker in West Virginia that would serve as a safe haven for top members of Congress, in the event of a catastrophe.[106] The project was similar in scope and intent to one initiated by President Truman in 1951. Called "Site R," that effort involved construction of an Alternate Joint Communications Center in Raven Rock Mountain, Pennsylvania, to be used in case existing centers in Washington, DC were destroyed by an attack.[107] Like his predecessor, Eisenhower believed it was vital for the government to ensure continuity of operations following an attack on the homeland. The West Virginia bunker was built under the five-star Greenbrier resort and was only placed on full alert once, during the Cuban Missile Crisis in 1962.[108] The public remained completely unaware of the operation until 1992 when the *Washington Post* broke the story.[109]

Kennedy Administration (1961-1963)

During the first year of his presidency, John F. Kennedy made civil defense more of a priority than at any previous time in U.S. history.[110] He was also the first President to discuss civil defense publicly, issuing an appeal in the September 7, 1961 issue of *LIFE* magazine to all Americans to protect themselves "and in doing so strengthen [the] nation."[111] Kennedy continued the approach of his predecessors of including civil defense in deterrence calculations, and he believed that the only effective deterrent was a strong retaliatory capability.[112] However, he also believed that deterrence could fail in the event one faced an irrational enemy, and thus a strong and coordinated approach to civil defense was required. As he stated to Congress on May 25, 1961:

> [Civil defense] can be readily justifiable…as insurance for the civilian population in case of an enemy

miscalculation. It is insurance we trust will never be needed – but insurance which we could never forgive ourselves for foregoing in the event of catastrophe.[113]

He concluded by proposing "a nationwide long-range program of identifying present fallout shelter capacity and providing shelter in new and existing structures."[114]

Photo Removed Due to Copyright Restrictions

The October 7, 1961 issue of
LIFE Magazine

To accomplish these goals, Kennedy issued Executive Order 10952 on July 20, 1961, which divided the Office of Civil Defense and Mobilization into two new organizations: the **Office of Emergency Planning** (OEP) and the **Office of Civil Defense**. OEP was part of the President's Executive Office and tasked with advising and assisting the President in determining policy for all *nonmilitary* emergency preparedness, including civil defense. OCD was part of the Office of the Secretary of Defense, and was tasked with overseeing the nation's civil defense program. The responsibility for carrying out the fallout shelter program was among the program operations assigned to Secretary of Defense Robert McNamara.[115]

The 1961 Berlin crisis gave Kennedy renewed urgency to improve US civil defense.[116] The President emphasized the importance of fallout shelters as a means to save lives.

He stressed that identifying and stocking existing shelters with food and medicine should be made a priority.[117] McNamara explained that this approach was not a major departure from the Eisenhower shelter program; however, the scope was larger and thus required more money.[118] The goal was to provide maximum protection through cost effective means by utilizing existing buildings. Some members of Congress, notably the ranking Republican of the House Appropriations Committee, John Taber, worked hard to limit funding to the shelter project. However, most underscored the importance of the shelter program as a rational response to the growing threat of a nuclear attack.[119] Congress ultimately approved more than $200 million that Kennedy asked for the project, which was twice as much as Eisenhower had ever requested for civil defense.[120]

With the appropriated funds, OCD began a nationwide survey of all existing shelters.[121] In order to be designated a public shelter, a facility had to have enough space for at least 50 people, include one cubic foot of storage space per person, and have a radiation protection factor of at least 100.[122] The materials division of DOD, called the Defense Supply Agency, furnished shelter supplies to local governments, which were then responsible for stocking all shelters in their regions.[123] By 1963, 104 million individual shelter spaces had been identified;[124] and of those 47 million had been licensed, 46 million marked, and 9 million individual spaces had been stocked with supplies.[125]

The President also decided to distribute booklets to the populace that would outline the purpose of the shelter program and the steps that every American should take during an attack. The booklet, created by a team of Madison Avenue writers, was to be sent to every household in the nation.[126] In an unintended twist, the booklets themselves created new controversy. Some presidential aides felt that the pictures used were too graphic, while others felt that they indicated the booklet was meant only for the upper class.[127] Ultimately the Kennedy Administration decided to tone down the content, so as not to cause unnecessary alarm.[128] The booklets were then sent to post offices throughout the nation, so people could pick up copies.

The means of communicating the Administration's civil defense message to the public was not the only target of controversy during this time. Reviving a long-standing debate,

The fallout shelter sign was introduced by DOD in December 1961 to indicate Federally-approved shelter space

some prominent members of Congress, including Albert Thomas, the Chairman of the House Appropriations Subcommittee in charge of civil defense, felt that the Federal government should not be undertaking such a massive sheltering project when civil defense responsibility belonged to State and local governments.[129] Kennedy convened a meeting with eighteen of his top advisors at Hyannis Port, Massachusetts, on the day after Thanksgiving in 1961 to discuss the appropriate next steps for civil defense.[130] There, consensus evolved that the Federal government's primary role was to provide community shelters.[131]

Johnson Administration (1963-1969)

Kennedy's assassination in November 1963 marked the beginning of a drastic cutback in funding of the Nation's civil defense program.

The topic began to fall slowly off the public radar, and President Lyndon B. Johnson allowed it to slip further by not pressuring Congress to pass the Shelter Incentive Program bill,[132] which proposed to give every non-profit institution financial compensation for each shelter it built.[133]

Earlier in the decade, Secretary McNamara had begun to describe the concept of "mutual assured destruction" (MAD), which essentially meant that the Soviet Union and the United States had the capacity to effectively annihilate one another with the weapons in their arsenals, such that this constituted an effective deterrent to offensive action.[134] Congress and the public began to accept the doctrine of MAD. As a result, a growing percentage of the population began to wonder if civil defense programs could adequately protect citizens from a large scale nuclear attack.[135] However, when the U.S. military began expanding its ABM defense system, McNamara re-emphasized the importance of a shelter system because he questioned the wisdom of relying solely on an ABM defense.[136] He argued that "the effectiveness of an ABM defense system in saving lives depends in large part upon the availability of adequate fallout shelters for the population."[137] The belief was that the ABM defense system could be beaten by detonating nuclear weapons upwind of large metropolitan areas and outside the range of the defensive missiles. The result would be radioactive fallout spreading across America's cities.[138] Large numbers of people would die from the exposure to the fallout, unless there were a sufficient number of shelters. Congress opposed financing a shelter system, and McNamara continued to be pessimistic about an ABM defense system saying, "Whether we will ever be able to advance the art of defense as rapidly as the art of offensive developments…I don't know. At the moment it doesn't look at all likely."[139]

In an ironic twist, attention to civil defense was also undermined by a series of major natural disasters that rattled the Nation. Hurricanes Hilda and Betsy devastated the Southeast, an Alaskan earthquake caused a damaging tidal wave in California, and a lethal tornado swept through Indiana on Palm Sunday in 1965.[140] Senator Birch Bayh of Indiana sponsored legislation that granted emergency Federal loan assistance to disaster victims.[141] The bill passed in 1966, and Bayh urged Congress over the next few years to provide even more disaster assistance to citizens. The concept of all-hazards assistance was gaining adherents, at the expense of civil preparedness for attack.[142]

The Vietnam War struck a further blow to civil defense during the Johnson years. As the war progressed, it required increasing amounts of time, money, and resources.[143] Although civil defense efforts continued to receive modest funding, and would for the next twelve years, no major steps were taken to enhance overall capabilities.[144] A transformation in the way the Federal government viewed the task of protecting the public had begun.

In Time of Emergency was quietly released in March of 1968, when the Vietnam War and domestic unrest effectively overshadowed civil defense planning.

Nixon Administration (1969-1974)

By the time President Nixon entered office, public and government interest in civil defense had fallen precipitously from its peak in the early 1960s. According to the *New York Times* Index, in 1968, only four articles on civil defense appeared in that publication compared to 72 in 1963.[145] However, the new administration did make a major contribution to civil defense by redefining civil defense policy to include preparedness for natural disasters. In no small measure, the President's thinking resulted from the Federal government's lack of preparedness to handle the horrific damage wrought by Hurricane Camille (see discussion below). Upon entering office, Nixon immediately tasked the OEP to complete a broad review of the Nation's civil defense programs.[146]

In June 1970, the OEP released the results of its comprehensive assessment in National Security Study Memorandum 57.[147] The study concluded that the Nation's preparedness for natural disasters was minimal to nonexistent.[148] The Administration responded by introducing two of its most significant domestic policy changes in National Security Decision Memorandum (NSDM) 184. NSDM 184 recommended the establishment of a "dual-use approach" to Federal citizen preparedness programs and the replacement of the Office of Civil Defense with the **Defense Civil Preparedness Agency** (DCPA).[149] President Nixon would later implement these recommendations, placing the new DCPA under the umbrella of the Department of Defense.

For the first time in the history of civil defense, Federal funds previously allocated for the exclusive purpose of preparing for military attacks could be shared with State and local governments for natural disaster preparedness. This dual-use initiative subscribed to the philosophy that preparations for evacuation, communications, and survival are common to both natural disasters and enemy military strikes on the homeland. From a practical perspective, the dual-use approach allowed more efficient utilization of limited resources, so planners could address a larger number of scenarios.[150] Given that civil defense funding during Nixon's first term barely exceeded the low $80 million per year level of the Eisenhower Administration (when adjusted for inflation), scarce resources likely played a part in the decision to adopt the new approach.[151]

A series of natural disasters during Nixon's tenure also increased the pressure to expand civil defense to include preparation and response to natural disasters. Several major hurricanes and earthquakes exposed significant flaws in natural disaster preparedness at a time when no centralized system for disaster relief existed.[152] Perhaps most significantly, in August 1969 Hurricane Camille wreaked havoc in the greater Gulf Coast region, highlighting major problems with disaster response.[153] In response, Congress passed the Disaster Relief Act of 1969, which created the concept of a Federal Coordinating Officer (FCO). The FCO was an individual appointed by the President, who would manage federal disaster assistance on-the-spot at a given disaster area.[154]

In 1972, the United States and the Soviet Union signed the SALT I treaty, an important arms control measure.

The President's decision to increase focus on natural disaster preparedness also aligned with

U.S. foreign policy considerations. In order to reinforce the doctrine of MAD, Nixon was deeply involved in negotiations with the Soviet Union to limit defensive weapon capabilities.[155] The first Strategic Arms Limitation Talks treaty (SALT I), signed on May 26, 1972, froze the number of strategic ballistic missile launchers and allowed the addition of new submarine ballistic missile launchers only as replacements for dismantled older launchers.[156] Perhaps most significantly, SALT I limited the superpowers to only two ABM defense deployment sites.[157] Advocates of SALT argued that such agreements were necessary because any increase in defense capabilities would spur another arms race for improved offensive capabilities.[158] The Nixon Administration felt that the SALT I advances would be jeopardized if either side continued to build up nuclear attack-related civil defense programs. This concern helped justify the decision to turn more attention toward civil preparedness for natural disasters.[159]

The dual use approach was attractive to State and local authorities. While in the past State and local officials had been reluctant to participate in nuclear attack planning, the ability to deal with attack preparedness in the context of a particular hazard in a specific area (e.g. floods in coastal or riverine areas, hurricanes in coastal areas, tornadoes in the Midwest and Plains States, and civil unrest in urban areas) encouraged new coordination and participation.[160]

The change of focus also garnered public support. The interest of the American public in attack planning had waned considerably. There was little enthusiasm for ambitious shelter building projects or evacuation drills.[161] A number of historians attribute this lack of interest to a diminished perception of risk, psychological numbing to the destruction of nuclear weapons, and a growing belief that civil defense measures would not ultimately be effective in the event of nuclear war.[162] Planning for natural disasters was perceived to be more effective, less resource intensive, and able to deliver tangible benefits at the State and local level.

Nixon's broad policy changes were accompanied by equally sweeping organizational changes. Following the replacement of the OCD with the DCPA, another major reorganization took place. In 1970 and 1973, Reorganization Plans 1 and 2 abolished the Office of Emergency Planning and delegated its functions to various agencies.[163] Executive Order 11725 of 1973 solidified the new organizational structure by distributing preparedness tasks to a wide variety of new agencies including the Department of Housing and Urban Development (HUD), the General Services Administration, and the Departments of the Treasury and Commerce.[164] In total, the new bureaucratic structure placed responsibility for disaster relief with more than 100 federal agencies.[165] Not surprisingly, this reorganization is perhaps best known for its ineffectiveness.[166]

Despite the suggestion of great activity, real progress on civil defense, both in the traditional sense and its new dual-use direction, was limited during the Nixon Administration. One illustrative example is the signing into law of the Disaster Relief Act of 1974 (Public Law 93-288). While the Disaster Relief Act sought to remedy bureaucratic inefficiencies and provide direct assistance to individuals and families following a disaster,[167] funding remained low, with levels comparable to spending in the pre-Kennedy years. The Act did succeed in involving State and local governments in all hazards preparedness activities[168] and provided matching funds for their programs.[169] However, soon the federal government's emphasis on all-hazards preparedness would lessen.

Ford Administration (1974-1977)

At first, the Ford Administration supported its predecessor's approach to dual-use preparedness. In March 1975 President Ford strongly endorsed the policy, stating: "I am particularly pleased that civil defense planning today emphasizes the dual use of resources…we are improving our ability to respond…to national disasters…"[170] However, less than a year later, the Office of Management and Budget (OMB) rescinded DOD's use of civil defense funding for natural disaster mitigation and preparedness.[171] Civil defense was returned to the original orientation of nuclear attack preparedness, as seen during the Truman and Eisenhower years.

There were several motivations for this policy change. Perhaps most importantly, the United States had just resumed its intelligence observations of Soviet civil defense after a five year break.[172] Reports from these operations detailed significant Soviet progress in civil defense, compared to relatively small U.S. efforts. Massive Soviet expenditures (estimated at $1 billion per year in 1977) on preparedness initiatives, such as evacuation plans, contributed to a growing concern that the United States was falling behind.[173] Whereas in the United States, civil defense was considered "an insurance policy," the Soviets considered it a "factor of great strategic significance."[174] The most alarmist American commentators concluded that the entire U.S. nuclear arsenal could not inflict significant damage on the Soviet Union, due in large part to its increased civil preparedness.[175]

Developments in Cold War diplomacy likely also contributed to the temporary end of all-hazards planning. Gradually the doctrine of MAD was replaced with new ideas, such as limited nuclear strikes against strategically important military and industrial targets, rather than population centers. As early as January 10, 1974 Secretary of Defense James Schlesinger stated during a press conference that "the old policy [of MAD]…was no longer adequate for deterrence" and should be replaced by "a set of selective options against different sets of targets."[176] Over the next decade, these ideas of flexible targeting and limited retaliation developed into the policy of "flexible response."[177] Flexible response was based on the idea that both the Soviet Union and the United States had the capability for small-scale nuclear attacks that could be answered by similarly-sized acts of retaliation by the other side.[178] Theoretically, instead of massive retaliation against population centers, targets would be specific, highly-strategic sites.[179] Since some of these sites could be civilian in nature, some level of civil defense and nuclear attack preparedness was deemed necessary. Thus, U.S. policy makers renewed their attention on civil defense, as a means of protecting against targeted highly-strategic attacks.[180]

Public relations officer presenting a crisis relocation plan.

One result was a new initiative called the **Crisis Relocation Plan** (CRP). Begun in 1974 by Secretary of Defense James Schlesinger, the CRP favored a strategy of evacuation rather than sheltering. Directed by the DCPA, CRP evacuation planning was conducted at the State level with Federal funds and encompassed all of the necessary

support for relocation, food distribution, and medical care.[181] Under the CRP, urban residents would be relocated to rural host counties, with a target ratio of "5 immigrants for every native."[182] The focus on preparedness through the CRP was continued throughout the Ford Administration by incoming Secretary of Defense Donald Rumsfeld, who strongly opposed the dual-use approach. Rumsfeld believed that the Federal government should address only attack preparedness, while peacetime disasters were a State and local responsibility.[183]

Though Administration officials and policymakers defended the CRP as a set of simple and highly effective procedures, the program suffered widespread criticism.[184] The Plan's reliance on a relatively long warning time (1 to 2 days), compared to the shorter notice necessary for sheltering, meant it could only be effective in a situation of rising tensions in which the launch of missiles against the country could be predicted. Additionally, vocal critics from Congress and the public doubted the feasibility of such large-scale evacuations through bottlenecked transportation routes.

Organizationally, the fragmentation of civil defense responsibilities begun under Nixon became increasingly apparent. Nixon's reorganization plans prescribed that the bulk of the responsibility for civil defense fall to three different agencies: the OEP would advise the President, HUD's **Federal Disaster Assistance Agency** would manage disaster relief, and the DCPA would coordinate State and local preparedness efforts.[185] Though these bureaucratic changes were not complete until the Carter Administration, some Congressional committees were already beginning to investigate the problem of disjointed civil defense. In 1976, the House Armed Services Committee recommended that an office within the Executive Office of the President (EOP) be tasked to manage civil defense, while the Joint Committee on Defense Production recommended combining the three agencies into one body.[186] These recommendations, coming during the final months of the Ford Administration, were evaluated in the subsequent Carter Administration.

Overall civil defense funding during Ford's tenure did not change significantly from the Nixon years. With the implementation of the CRP, Secretary of Defense Schlesinger made modest increases in the 1975 budget to develop city evacuation plans and implement population defenses.[187] However, as in previous Administrations, civil defense still competed for funding against more traditional military expenditures, and the 1975 increases were nullified the following year in favor of spending on offensive military capabilities.[188]

In sum, despite ambitious claims of progress by the Ford Administration, civil defense programs within the United States remained less than effective. U.S. nuclear deterrence plans still emphasized offensive capabilities. In its evaluation of the state of civil defense in 1976, the Congressional Research Service unconditionally labeled the efforts "a charade."[189] It would be another five years before significant progress was made.

Carter Administration (1977-1981)

Upon taking office, President Carter immediately began a review of the disjointed system of bureaucracies that managed civil defense. An interagency study led to Presidential Review Memorandum 32 in September of 1977.[190] The study concurred with the 1976 recommendations of the House Armed Services Committee and Joint Committee on Defense Production that the various civil defense agencies must be combined into one coherent agency in direct contact with the White House.[191] In response, Carter issued Presidential Directive (PD) 41 in September of 1978, which sought to clarify the Administration's view of civil defense. However, it did not offer any particular plan for implementation.[192] According to PD 41, civil defense was an element in the strategy to "enhance deterrence and stability". Civil defense still did not become a priority for the Administration, which concluded that it was not necessary to pursue "equivalent survivability" with the Soviet Union.[193]

Meanwhile, in the midst of a lengthy debate regarding the creation of a single disaster preparedness agency, an unprecedented civilian nuclear accident unfolded on March 28, 1979 at the nuclear energy plant on Three Mile Island, near Harrisburg, Pennsylvania.[194] By highlighting the slow response, poor local-Federal coordination, and miscommunications that occurred; the accident dramatically demonstrated the need for more effective disaster coordination and planning.[195] Partially in response to the near nuclear disaster, on July 20, 1979 the Administration issued Executive Order 12148, which established the **Federal Emergency Management Agency** (FEMA) as the lead agency for coordinating Federal disaster relief efforts. FEMA absorbed the Federal Insurance Administration, the National Fire Prevention and Control Administration, the National Weather Service Community Preparedness Program, the Federal Preparedness Agency of the General Services Administration, and the Federal Disaster Assistance Administration activities from HUD, and combined them into a single independent agency. At the time, the creation of FEMA represented the single largest consolidation of civil defense efforts in U.S. history.

Photo Removed Due to Copyright Restrictions

Conflicting official statements, skepticism about the nuclear industry, and even unfamiliar terminology fed the sensationalist media frenzy surrounding the Three Mile Island accident.

Despite the reorganization and move toward greater mission clarity, civil defense planning on the ground did not change dramatically. Practical plans continued to reflect traditional civil defense programs and did not adopt the dual-use approach, though Carter did urge FEMA to direct more of its efforts to coping with peacetime disasters.[196] Evacuation continued to be the focus of Federal planners, and Secretary of Defense Harold Brown reaffirmed his predecessor's crisis relocation strategies.[197] When FEMA assumed responsibility for citizen preparedness, the agency called on civil defense planners nationwide to create area-specific CRPs.[198]

The decision to continue to pursue evacuation as the primary civil defense policy was influenced by several factors. Well-funded and extensive Soviet evacuation programs continued to worry key U.S. decision makers, including Brown.[199] Evacuation also made sense in the context of continued resource limitations. According to a 1979 FEMA report, since effective and cost-efficient sheltering in large cities had proven difficult, "the U.S. nuclear civil defense program developed into an evacuation program…as a low-cost survival alternative."[200]

It is likely that the Carter Administration's focus on evacuation was also affected by Cold War diplomacy. The continuing SALT negotiations created a conflict between the desire to advance U.S. civil defense, and the desire to avoid upsetting the delicate strategic balance required for successful threat reduction negotiations. With this balance in mind, maintaining the status quo by continuing to support evacuation policies may have been deemed the best option.[201]

Though the creation of FEMA and the goals of PD 41 signaled renewed interest in civil defense, funding throughout the Carter Administration remained historically low. The 1980 request for $108 million was less than adequate for implementing the new plans.[202] In the following year, Congress did not meet a higher request for funding, instead choosing to allocate funds to other priorities.[203] As had been the case many times before, funding levels did not match the ambitious plans for program improvement.

In keeping civil defense funding low, Congressional leaders had little public opposition to fear. In contrast to generally widespread public participation and acceptance in the peak years of civil defense during the early stages of the Cold War, most people by this time had little faith that any government civil defense planning could lessen the impact of nuclear war.[204] Some local communities refused outright to cooperate with Federal civil defense mandates because they did not believe the CRPs would be effective if a nuclear attack were to occur.[205] This public attitude would continue throughout the remainder of the Cold War period.

Reagan Administration (1981-1989)

It would appear that Ronald Reagan entered office with the intention of building upon the civil defense foundations set by his predecessors. In December 1981, Congress acted dramatically in favor of the dual-use approach by amending the 1950 Civil Defense Act. In this milestone decision, all future civil defense funds would be allotted for natural disasters, as well as attacks on the homeland.[206] The amendment did stipulate that funding and planning for peacetime disasters could not overtly detract from attack preparedness programs. Nevertheless, dual-use preparedness was promoted with much of the same language and reasoning as it was during the Nixon Administration. [207]

Though Reagan was in favor of the dual-use approach, his civil defense strategy was largely a continuation of Carter's. In the midst of deliberations regarding the 1982 budget, the National Security Council (NSC) compiled National Security Division Directive (NSDD) 26, which spelled out the objectives of Carter's Presidential Directive 41 and was designed to promote deterrence, improve natural disaster preparedness, and reduce the possibility of coercion by enemy forces.[208] The unclassified version of NSDD 26 states: "it is a matter of national priority that the United States have a Civil Defense program which provides for the survival of the U.S. population."[209] However, NSDD 26 went further than PD 41 by stipulating a concrete deadline in 1989 for plans to protect the population, and it mandated that civil defense leaders investigate and enhance protection measures for critical industries in case of attack.[210] Furthermore, NSDD 26 for the first time supported research into the development of strategies to ensure economic survival in the event of a nuclear attack.[211] However, drawing upon the CRPs of his predecessors, Reagan continued to promote evacuation as

the primary strategy for civil defense. During this period nuclear preparedness became a top priority for FEMA.[212]

Congress and the Administration came into conflict in February 1982, when the President requested $4.2 billion for a seven-year plan to massively boost civil defense programs.[213] Congress did not react positively to this request, particularly because it seemed to be part of Reagan's hawkish stance on Cold War diplomacy.[214] For example, the House Committee on Appropriations criticized FEMA's dependence on evacuation planning at the expense of other preparedness programs and suggested that more attention be paid to peacetime disaster preparation. Expressing their disagreement with FEMA's plans, Congress allocated only $147.9 million to cover FEMA's 1983 budget, about 58% of what the agency had requested.[215] In 1984 and 1985, Congress again blocked requests for funding increases.[216]

In 1983, FEMA responded to the Congressional push for more peacetime disaster preparation with plans for an Integrated Emergency Management System (IEMS) to develop full all-hazard preparedness plans at the Federal level.[217] Under the IEMS, State civil defense planners would facilitate the development of multi-hazard preparedness plans based on threats faced by specific localities.[218] According to the IEMS, this all-hazards approach included "direction, control and warning systems which are common to the full range of emergencies from small isolated events to the ultimate emergency – war."[219] Despite this innovative attempt to integrate civil defense and disaster preparedness concerns, Congress was not sufficiently convinced that the IEMS would effectively address the management of all-hazard preparedness, and therefore never met requested FEMA funding levels.

Cold War diplomacy continued to play a role in civil defense decisions under Reagan. President Reagan supported neither the doctrine of mutual assured destruction nor the détente that had been a centerpiece of the Carter Administration.[220] On March 23, 1983 Reagan openly rejected mutual assured destruction with his speech proposing the Strategic Defense Initiative (SDI). SDI

1983 Time Magazine cover story reports on SDI. Labeled "Star Wars" by critics, the initiative was a firm departure from previous policies.

focused on using ground-based and space-based systems to protect the United States from attack by strategic nuclear ballistic missiles.[221] SDI flew in the face of the 1972 SALT I agreement banning strategic defenses, and it demonstrated a shift towards more proactive and aggressive defensive measures.

The final years of the Reagan Administration saw a number of actions intended to allay concerns regarding non-attack preparedness. The *Meese Memorandum* (Executive Order 12656), signed in 1986, delegated lead response roles to certain Federal agencies, depending on the type of disaster.[222] On November 23, 1988 the Disaster Relief Act of 1974 was amended to become what is now known as the Stafford Act, resulting in a clearer definition of FEMA's role in emergency management. The Act defined the disaster declaration process and provided the statutory authority for Federal assistance during a disaster. The agency's role in disaster response would be tested and debated in the years to come.

Bush Administration (1989-1993)

In the year after George H.W. Bush took office, several natural disasters challenged the Nation's nascent approach to all-hazards preparedness. On March 24, 1989, 11 million gallons of crude oil spilled into Prince William Sound in the Gulf of Alaska from the *Exxon Valdez* oil tanker.[223] It was the largest oil spill in U.S. history, and the Administration was ill-prepared to manage an environmental crisis of such large scale. Instead of using FEMA through the Stafford Act to coordinate the response, Bush invoked the Federal Water Pollution Control Act, under which the Environmental Protection Agency and Coast Guard managed the event. The Administration drew much criticism for the poor response.[224]

On September 13, 1989, Hurricane Hugo struck the Virgin Islands, Puerto Rico, and South Carolina, inflicting significant damage. This time Bush chose to send Manuel Lujan, Secretary of the Interior, to assess the damage and provide additional executive oversight.[225] FEMA's participation in the response was plagued by shortages of properly trained personnel, communication problems, and a lack of coordination.[226] Within a month of Hurricane Hugo, the Loma Prieta earthquake struck northern California causing an estimated $6 billion in damage. Already stretched thin from dealing with the Hurricane Hugo recovery, FEMA's response continued to be hindered by coordination and staffing problems. Again, President Bush appointed a Cabinet-level representative, Secretary of Transportation Samuel Skinner, to oversee recovery operations, and again FEMA's contribution to response and recovery was judged inadequate.[227]

The dissatisfaction with FEMA's response to the *Exxon Valdez* Oil Spill, Hurricane Hugo, and the Loma Prieta Earthquake led FEMA to begin developing the Federal Response

Plan (FRP) in November 1990.[228] Drawing from the Incident Command System and Incident Management System framework, the FRP defined how 27 Federal agencies and the American Red Cross would respond to the needs of State and local governments when they were overwhelmed by a disaster. The plan used a functional approach to define the types of assistance (such as food, communications, and transportation) that would be provided by the Federal government to address the consequences of disaster.[229]

By the second year of the Bush administration, significant political changes were occurring. The Berlin Wall fell in 1989, followed shortly by the collapse of the Soviet Union and the fall of communist governments across Eastern Europe. The Cold War had come to a rapid and unanticipated end, and the threat of a strategic nuclear attack on the United States diminished significantly almost overnight. As a result, civil defense in the traditional sense was no longer a major priority for emergency planners or Congress. With the recent onslaught of natural and man-made disasters top-of-mind, FEMA planners began to adopt the idea of a true all-hazards approach to disaster preparedness. In March of 1992, President Bush signed National Security Directive 66 instructing FEMA to develop a multi-hazard approach to emergency management, combining civil defense preparedness with natural and man-made disaster preparedness.[230]

Testifying before the Armed Services Subcommittee Hearing on Civil Defense on May 6, 1992, Grant Peterson, Associate Director for State and Local Programs at FEMA, reported that:

> [T]he President has approved a new civil defense policy…The new policy acknowledges significant changes in the range of threats, and eliminates the heavy emphasis on nuclear attack. The policy recognizes the need for civil defense to address all forms of catastrophic emergencies, all hazards, and the consequences of those hazards. The new policy increases the emphasis on preparedness to respond to the consequences of all emergencies regardless of their cause. All-hazards consequence management recognizes that regardless of the cause of an emergency situation, certain very basic capabilities are necessary to respond and that planning efforts and resources should be focused on developing the capabilities necessary to respond to all the common effects of all hazards.[231]

In August 1992, Hurricane Andrew hit south Florida and the central Louisiana coast. President Bush once again appointed a Cabinet-level representative, Secretary of Transportation Andrew Card, to coordinate Federal relief efforts.[232] Unfortunately, this additional oversight did not result in improved performance as "government at all levels was slow to comprehend the scope of the disaster."[233] And despite the presence of the FRP, FEMA and the other agencies involved in the response and recovery faced the same kinds of coordination and logistical problems they had three years prior. FEMA was strongly criticized by Congress for its poor performance.

As a result of this criticism, FEMA was instructed by Congress to contract with the National Academy of Public Administration (NAPA) to conduct a study of the Federal, State, and local level capacity to respond to major natural disasters.[234] Issued in February 1993, NAPA's assessment, *Coping With Catastrophe*, detailed the obstacles facing emergency management at all levels of government and made recommendations to improve FEMA's ability to prepare and respond to disasters. NAPA concluded that, "a small independent agency could coordinate the federal response to major natural disasters...but only if the White House and Congress take significant steps to make it a viable institution."[235] Because of the timing of the report, it was left to the Clinton Administration to evaluate the findings and implement changes to make FEMA more effective.

Clinton Administration (1993-2001)

Upon taking office, President Bill Clinton appointed James Lee Witt director of FEMA. Witt, the former Director of Emergency Management for the State of Arkansas, immediately reorganized FEMA.[236] He created three functional directorates corresponding to the major phases of emergency management: Mitigation; Preparedness; Training and Exercise; and Response and Recovery.[237] In February of 1996, Clinton elevated the FEMA directorship to Cabinet-level status, improving the line of communication between the Director and the President.[238]

The shift in emergency preparedness towards an all-hazards approach allowed FEMA to focus on addressing natural disasters without having to fear negative political reactions from advocates of civil defense.[239] The Agency's Mitigation Directorate, for example, focused many of its early programs on hazards such as flooding and earthquakes.[240] At the same time, however, recognition of the threat of terrorist attacks inside the United States was beginning to emerge. In 1993, Congress included a joint resolution in the National Defense Authorization Act (NDAA) that called for FEMA to develop "a capability for early detection and warning of and response to: potential terrorist use of chemical or biological agents or weapons; and emergencies or natural disasters involving

industrial chemicals or the widespread outbreak of disease."[241]

As evidenced by this resolution, Congress was becoming increasingly concerned about the threat posed by terrorist organizations and technological disasters. Much of this concern resulted from the World Trade Center bombing earlier that year, in which 6 people were killed and 1,042 were wounded. The blast left a five story deep crater and caused $500 million in damages.

In November 1994, the Federal Civil Defense Act of 1950 was repealed and all remnants of civil defense authority were transferred to Title VI of the Stafford Act.[242] This completed the evolution of civil defense into an all-hazards approach to preparedness. FEMA now had the statutory responsibility for coordinating a comprehensive emergency preparedness system to deal with all types of disasters. Title VI also ended all Armed Services Committee oversight over FEMA and significantly reduced the priority of national security programs within FEMA. Money authorized by the Civil Defense Act was reallocated to natural disaster and all-hazards programs, and more than 100 defense and security staff members were reassigned.[243]

The period between 1995 and 1996 saw a series of major terrorist attacks launched domestically and abroad, which further influenced U.S. preparedness policies. In March 1995, the Japanese religious cult Aum Shinrikyo released sarin nerve gas on five separate cars of three different subway lines in Tokyo. Twelve people were killed and thousands were injured. One month later, Timothy McVeigh and Terry Nichols detonated a truck bomb at the Alfred P. Murrah Federal Building in Oklahoma City, killing 169 people. On June 25, 1996 the Khobar Towers, a U.S. military facility in Dhahran, Saudi Arabia was bombed, killing 19 Americans.[244]

23

These events had a profound effect on U.S. lawmakers and the Administration.[245] Two days after the bombing of the Khobar Towers, the Senate adopted an amendment aimed at preventing terrorists from using nuclear, chemical, or biological weapons in the United States.[246] In September Congress passed the NDAA for fiscal year 1997, which included the Defense Against Weapons of Mass Destruction Act commonly known as the Nunn-Lugar-Domenici Act.[247] This Act required DOD to provide civilian agencies at all levels of government training and expert advice on appropriate responses to the use of a weapon of mass destruction (WMD) against the American public. Lawmakers originally planned to have FEMA lead the training and provide equipment; however, FEMA officials had testified that only DOD had the necessary knowledge and assets .[248]

As a result of the Nunn-Lugar-Domenici legislation, Metropolitan Medical Strike Force Teams were created, as well as a domestic terrorism rapid response team, whose purpose was to aid State and local officials in WMD response.[249] Three years later, WMD preparedness was transferred from DOD to the **Office of Domestic Preparedness** (ODP) within the Department of Justice (DOJ).[250] In 1999, DOD also established 10 National Guard Rapid Assessment and Initial Detection (RAID) teams, which served to provide technical expertise and equipment to deal with a WMD attack.[251] The unanticipated result of these actions was a new fragmentation of responsibility for civilian preparedness programs. Despite its overtures toward all-hazards preparedness, many of FEMA's efforts remained focused on natural disasters. Meanwhile, DOD through its RAID teams, and DOJ through ODP, became increasingly involved in preparations for and responses to WMD threats.

Apart from these efforts, as the century came to a close, a new concept of homeland security began to emerge. Presidential Decision Directive (PDD) 62, signed in May 1998, created the **Office of the National Coordinator for Security, Infrastructure Protection, and Counter-Terrorism** within the Executive Office of the President. This office was designed to coordinate counter-terrorism policy, preparedness, and consequence management.[252]

Later that same year, President Clinton issued PDD 63 on Critical Infrastructure Protection. PDD 63 established principles for protecting the nation by minimizing the threat of smaller-scale terrorist attacks against information technology and geographically-distributed supply chains that could cascade and disrupt entire sectors of the economy.[253] In the absence of a centralized authority for homeland security, Federal agencies were designated as lead agencies in their sector of expertise. The lead agencies were directed to develop sector-specific Information Sharing and Analysis Centers to coordinate efforts with the private sector. PDD 63 also required the creation of a National Infrastructure Assurance Plan.

At the same time, the **U.S. Commission on National Security in the 21st Century**, chartered by DOD, and known as the Hart-Rudman Commission, began to reexamine U.S. national security policies.[254] One of the Commission's recommendations was the creation of a Cabinet-level National Homeland Security Agency responsible for planning, coordinating, and integrating various U.S. government activities involved in "homeland security". The commission defined homeland security as "the protection of the territory, critical infrastructures, and citizens of the United States by Federal, State, and local government entities from the threat or use of chemical, biological, radiological, nuclear, cyber, or conventional weapons by military or other means." Legislation toward this end was introduced on March 29, 2001, but hearings continued through April of 2001 without passage of the legislation.[255]

Another influential commission formed during the latter stages of the Clinton Administration was the Gilmore Commission, chaired by Virginia Governor Jim Gilmore. The Commission, officially known as the **Advisory Panel to Assess Domestic Response Capabilities for Terrorism Involving Weapons of Mass Destruction**, developed and delivered a series of five reports to the President and Congress between 1999 and 2003.[256] Of the Gilmore Commission's 164 recommendations, 146 were adopted in whole or in part[257], including creation of a fusion center to integrate and analyze all intelligence pertaining to terrorism and counterterrorism and the creation of a civil liberties oversight board.[258] However, the impetus to implement many of these recommendations only occurred following the series of devastating attacks on the U.S. homeland that occurred during the initial months of the next administration.

Funding for Homeland Security
FY 1995 through FY 2003 Request

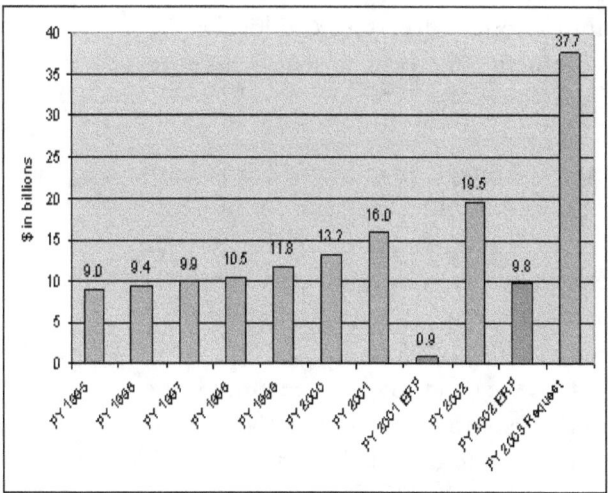

Levels for FY 1995 through FY 1997 are estimated, as OMB did not collect data on these activities prior to FY 1998.

Bush Administration (2001-Present)

The initial months of George W. Bush's presidency saw a general continuation of existing homeland security policies. Prior to the terrorist attacks of September 11, 2001, OMB summarized homeland security as focused on three objectives: counterterrorism, defense against WMD, and the protection of critical infrastructure.[259]

The new Administration did implement changes that affected how national security and homeland security policies would be generated. The Administration abolished the system of *ad hoc* interagency working groups used by Clinton to address homeland security issues and replaced them with Policy Coordination Committees within the National Security Council. A **Counterterrorism and National Preparedness Policy Coordinating Committee** was established that was composed of four working groups: Continuity of Federal Operations, Counterterrorism and Security, Preparedness and WMD, and Information Infrastructure Protection and Assurance.[260] The goal of this reorganization was to create a more formalized structure to deal with threats to the homeland.

Then came the September 11, 2001 terrorist attacks. In their wake, there was near-universal agreement within the Federal government that homeland security required a major reassessment, increased funding, and administrative reorganization. In October 2001, the White House **Office of Homeland Security** was established via executive order to work with Executive departments and agencies to develop and coordinate the implementation of a comprehensive national strategy to secure the United States from terrorist threats or attacks.[261] President Bush chose Pennsylvania Governor Tom Ridge to lead the new Office. In March 2002 another executive order created the **Homeland Security Advisory Council** to advise the President on homeland security matters. The Council, located within the Executive Office of the President, is comprised of leaders from State and local government, first responder communities, the private sector, and academia.

In his 2002 State of the Union address, the President announced the establishment of the **USA Freedom Corps** to promote a culture of service, citizenship, and responsibility in America. Under the Freedom Corps initiative, the White House established **Citizen Corps** within FEMA to engage individual citizens through education, training, and volunteer service to make communities better prepared to prevent, protect, respond, and recover from all-hazards. Citizen Corps involved Americans in programs such as Community Emergency Response Teams, Fire Corps, Neighborhood Watch, Medical Reserve Corps, and Volunteers in Police Service.

Then on March 12, 2002, the **Homeland Security Advisory System** (HSAS) was created to communicate with the American public and safety officials using a threat-based, color-coded system, so protective measures can be implemented to reduce the likelihood or impact of an attack on the homeland.[262] Because raising the threat condition can have detrimental economic, physical, and psychological effects on the nation, the Federal government can place specific geographic regions or industry sectors on a higher alert status, as the specificity of threat-based intelligence permits.[263]

.

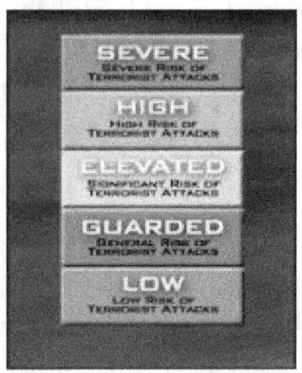

Homeland Security Advisory System

The Bush Administration also began to develop a number of strategic documents and statements that outlined the President's vision for protecting the nation. These included the National Security Strategy, the **National Strategy for Homeland Security** (NSHS), and the National Strategy to Combat Weapons of Mass Destruction.

The NSHS was released by the Office of Homeland Security, and its purpose was "to provide a framework to align the resources of the federal budget directly to the task of securing the homeland" against terrorist attack.[264] The NSHS was a comprehensive strategic document that advanced six critical mission areas: intelligence and warning, border and transportation security, domestic counterterrorism, protecting critical infrastructure, defending against catastrophic terrorism, and emergency preparedness and response. Importantly, the NSHS gave the proposed **Department of Homeland Security** (DHS) "a central role" in implementing the NSHS and directed the new department to "serve as the primary federal point of contact for state and local governments, the private sector, and the American people."[265]

As these strategic plans were being developed, Congress continued to push for more substantial reorganization of the Federal agencies involved in homeland security. A bipartisan group of Senate and House members proposed an ambitious new Department of Homeland Security. The President submitted his own plan for the creation of a homeland security department on June 6, 2002. The Homeland Security Act of 2002 established the new Department on November 25, 2002, and the President named Ridge its first Secretary in January 2003.

The official seal of DHS was
unveiled on June 19, 2003

As the head of a Cabinet-level department, Ridge obtained increased budgetary authority and control over many of the agencies involved in homeland security. In the largest government reorganization since the creation of DOD in the late 1940s, DHS inherited approximately 200,000 people from 22 Federal agencies, and an initial budget of $37 billion.[266]

One of the first major initiatives of the newly created DHS was the release of its citizen preparedness website, *Ready.gov*, in February 2003. The *Ready Campaign* began a national public service advertising campaign produced by The Ad Council in partnership with DHS designed to educate and empower Americans to prepare for and respond to natural disasters and potential terrorist attacks.[267]

DHS also began addressing priority issues of transportation, border, and port security. Steps to bolster aviation security included deploying newly trained federal screeners at airports and placing thousands of federal air marshals on flights to protect passengers and crew.[268] Also, Ridge oversaw a significant expansion of the Container Security Initiative. In less than a year, the United States was working with allies in 17 international ports to inspect and secure the thousands of containers of cargo that arrive daily at U.S. shores.[269]

Understandably, much of the Department's initial work focused on addressing the threat of domestic terrorism. However, the DHS mandate encompassed the full range of disasters and attacks, and all-hazards

preparedness soon became a top priority as well. Homeland Security Presidential Directive-8: National Preparedness (HSPD-8), issued in December 2003, defined preparedness as encompassing "threatened or actual domestic terrorist attacks, major disasters, and other emergencies." [270] HSPD-8 also spelled out the need for DHS to take a leading role in creating a National Preparedness Goal; coordinating Federal, State, local, and private sector efforts to encourage active citizen participation in preparedness; and developing a comprehensive plan to provide accurate and timely preparedness information to citizens.[271]

The National Preparedness Goal was first released in interim form on March 31, 2005. It presented preparedness as a coordinated, national effort involving every level of government, the private sector, non-governmental organizations, and individual citizens, and called for the development and strengthening of capabilities that would address the full range of homeland security missions (prevention, protection, response and recovery).

Under Ridge, DHS took a fresh look at the way Federal, State, local, tribal and private sector resources work together to deal with emergencies. A new National Response Plan (NRP) was developed to replace the earlier Federal Response Plan, and the National Incident Management System (NIMS) was introduced to provide a common framework for incident management. A National Strategy for Physical Protection of Critical Infrastructures and Key Assets was also developed, officially recognizing the role of the private sector and the need for partnerships between government and the private sector in protecting the nation. The structure for such partnerships was further detailed in the National Infrastructure Protection Plan, issued in June 2006.

Preparedness took on even greater prominence within the Department under Ridge's successor, Michael Chertoff. Shortly after taking office in February 2005, Chertoff initiated a Second Stage Review of the Department's organization, operations, and policies. The following six-point agenda resulted from the review: increase preparedness with a focus on catastrophic events; strengthen border security and interior enforcement and reform immigration processes; harden transportation security without sacrificing mobility; enhance information sharing with our U.S. government and private sector partners; improve DHS financial, human resource, procurement and information technology management; and realign the DHS organization to maximize mission performance.[272] The review also resulted in the creation of a new **Directorate of Preparedness** and further integration of preparedness activities.

The Nation's preparedness received another serious test when on August 29, 2005, Hurricane Katrina made landfall along the Mississippi and Louisiana coasts. The storm was followed by levee failures in New Orleans, and caused unprecedented devastation. With virtually the entire Mississippi coast leveled by storm surge, and much of the city of New Orleans under water, the Federal, State, and local response proved inadequate to the unprecedented catastrophic challenge. The National Response Plan, aimed at coordinating the response to major disasters, was less than one year old when the hurricane hit. It had not been fully trained across all agencies and levels of government, and had never been tested in a major event. The White House, Senate, and House of Representatives' investigative reports written in the months following the hurricane's landfall cited numerous shortcomings in response efforts.

State and local level preparedness for the disaster also proved to be flawed. President Bush, recognizing the importance of having adequate plans in place, demanded a nationwide review of the status of catastrophic planning. DHS and the Department of Transportation were tasked to conduct the review in major urban areas across the country.

The results were released on June 16, 2006. The Review determined that disaster planning for catastrophic events in the United States suffers from failure to account for the full scope of catastrophic events; outmoded planning processes, products, and tools; and inadequate attention to coordination.

While recognizing the importance of Federal leadership and coordination, DHS and the Bush Administration continue to stress that State and local governments must be the first line of defense against disaster and attack. DHS administers grant programs that since 2003 have provided over $2.1 billion to States for interoperable communications equipment, planning, training, and exercises.[273] In total, DHS has awarded $18 billion in grants to State and local governments to improve preparedness levels.[274] DHS has also provided counterterrorism training to more than 1.2 million emergency response personnel from across the country on a range of incident response issues such as incident management, unified command, and public works protection and response.[275] Finally, the Department has conducted more than 400 exercises at the Federal, State, and local level to improve preparedness for and response to terrorist attacks and natural disasters.[276]

Conclusion

The history of civil defense and homeland security in the United States has been one of frequent policy and organizational change.

The changes have been driven by many factors including an evolving threat environment, major natural disasters that have resulted in immense destruction, and the specific preferences of presidential administrations. One of the most important recent drivers, the terrorist attacks of September 11, 2001, led directly to increased funding and focus on homeland security, and specifically the creation of DHS. However, just a few years later, the scale of the devastation caused by Hurricane Katrina showed that the country remains vulnerable to natural disasters, as well as to manmade accidents.

Civil defense began with the desire to involve Americans in the protection of their fellow citizens and critical infrastructure from destruction at the hands of our enemies, and evolved over time to encompass coordinated, professional efforts, involving all levels of government, the private sector, and citizens, to address a wide range of disaster and attack scenarios. As the nation's population growth and economic development have put more and more people, property, and infrastructure at risk, and as the political importance of national preparedness has grown, the scope of preparedness efforts is likely to continue to expand.

Endnotes

1 "Strategic Bombing in World War I – Germany." Electronic Encyclopedia of Civil Defense and Emergency Management. Retrieved 6/2006 from http://www.richmond.edu/~wgreen/ECDstratbombIge.html
2 *Ibid.*
3 Thomas J. Kerr (1983). *Civil Defense in the U.S., Bandaid for a Holocaust?* (Westview Press, Inc., 1983). P. 10.
4 "Strategic Bombing". Electronic Encyclopedia.
5 Kerr. 11.
6 "Records of the Council of National Defense". The National Archives. Retrieved 6/2006 from http://www.archives.gov/research/guide-fed-records/groups/062.html
7 "Council of National Defense". Washington Watchdog. Retrieved 6/2006 from http://www.washingtonwatchdog.org/documents/usc/ttl50/ch1/sec1.html
8 "Records of the Council of National Defense".
9 "World War I- Council of Defense". Nevada State Library and Archives. Retrieved 6/2006 from http://dmla.clan.lib.nv.us/DOCS/NSLA/archives/archival/spboards/cdwwi.htm
10 "Records of the Council of National Defense".
11 Kerr. 13.
12 "Text of Executive Order 6443A: November 17, 1933". The Creation of the National Emergency Council. Retrieved 6/2006 from http://www.uhuh.com/laws/donncoll/eo/1933/EO6433A.TXT "Text of Executive Order 6899: October 31, 1934". The American Presidency Project. Retrieved 6/2006 from http://www.presidency.ucsb.edu/ws/index.php?pid=14769&st=&st1=
13 *Ibid.*
14 Kerr. 13.
15 Kerr. 14.
16 Elwyn A. Mauck (1946). *Civilian Defense in the United States: 1940-1945.* (Unpublished manuscript by the Historical Officer of the Office of Civilian Defense, July 1946). P. 55.
17 Allida Back, June Hopkins, et al. (Eds.) (2003). *Teaching Eleanor Roosevelt.* (Hyde Park, New York: Eleanor Roosevelt National Historic Site 2003). Retrieved 6/2006 from http://www.nps.gov/elro/glossary/office-civilian-defense.htm
18 *Ibid.*
19 Kerr. 16.
20 Laura McEnaney (2000). *Civil Defense Begins at Home: Militarization Meets Everyday Life in the Fifties.* (Princeton University Press 2000). P. 16
21 McEnaney. 17.
22 Kerr. 16-17.
23 Kerr. 18.
24 Kerr. 19.
25 "Office of Civilian Defense". Eleanor Roosevelt National Historic Site. Retrieved 6/2006 from http://www.nps.gov/elro/glossary/office-civilian-defense.htm
26 Lawrence J. Vale (1987). *The Limits of Civil Defence in the USA, Switzerland, Britain and the Soviet Union.* (Macmillan Press 1987). P. 58.
27 B. Wayne Blanchard (1986). "American Civil Defense 1945-1984: The Evolution of Programs and Policies." *Federal Emergency Management Agency Monograph Series, National Emergency Center Emmitsburg, Maryland:* Vol. 2: Issue No. 2 (July 1986). P. 1-29.
28 Kerr. 19.
29 Kerr. 20.
30 Kerr. 21.
31 Vale. 59.
32 *Ibid.*
33 "Text of the National Security Act of 1947". Retrieved 6/2006 from http://www.iwar.org.uk/sigint/resources/national-security-act/1947-act.htm

34 Kerr. 22.
35 *Ibid.*
36 "SEMP Biot #243: What is Civil Defense?" Suburban Emergency Management Project. Retrieved 6/2006 from http://www.semP.us/biots/biot_243.html
37 Kerr. 23.
38 *Ibid.*
39 Kerr. 24.
40 "SEMP Biota #243: What is Civil Defense?"
41 Kerr. 24.
42 Kerr. 25.
43 *Ibid.*
44 Kerr. 26.
45 *Ibid.*
46 Vale. 59.
47 Blanchard. 3.
48 Kerr. 27-28.
49 McEnaney. 20.
50 McEnaney. 25.
51 *Ibid.*
52 Andrew D. Grossman (2001). *Neither Dead nor Red.* (Routledge 2001). P. 41-42.
53 JoAnne Brown (1988). "A is for Atom, B is for Bomb: Civil Defense in American Public Education, 1948-1963". *The Journal of American History:* Vol. 75, No. 1. (June 1988). P. 68-90.
54 "Duck and Cover". CONELRAD. Retrieved 06/2006 from http://www.conelrad.com/duckandcover/cover.php?turtle=04
55 *Ibid.*
56 *Ibid.*
57 *Ibid.*
58 "Librarian of Congress Adds 25 films to National Film Registry". Library of Congress. Retrieved 06/2006 from http://www.loc.gov/today/pr/2004/04-215.html
59 Laura McEnaney. "Interview: The Message of Self-Help". PBS Special: The American Experience-- Race for the Superbomb. Retrieved 06/2006 from http://www.pbs.org/wgbh/amex/bomb/filmmore/reference/interview/mcenaney03.html
60 Kerr. 47.
61 *Ibid.*
62 Blanchard. 3.
63 McEnaney. 28
64 McEnaney. 25
65 Kerr. 30.
66 Kerr. 60.
67 Vale. 61.
68 "Chart of Civil Defense Budgets and Appropriations". *The American Civil Defense Association Alert.* November 1984.
69 Blanchard. 7.
70 Blanchard. 7.
71 Kerr. 61.
72 Kerr. 64.
73 Blanchard. 4.
74 *Ibid.*
75 Kerr. 67.
76 *Ibid.*
77 "View from the Bunker: Stock Up". Chico State. Retrieved 06/2006 from http://www.csuchico.edu/pub/inside/archive/03_04_03/01_bunker.html
78 Kerr. 68.
79 "The Bravo Test". PBS Special: The American Experience-Race for the Superbomb. Retrieved 06/2006 from http://www.pbs.org/wgbh/amex/bomb/peopleevents/pandeAMEX51.html
80 Vale. 61-62.
81 Blanchard. 5.
82 Kerr. 77.
83 *Ibid.*
84 Kerr. 78.

[85] *Ibid.*
[86] Kerr. 79.
[87] Kerr. 82.
[88] *Ibid.*
[89] *Ibid.*
[90] *Ibid.*
[91] Kerr. 94.
[92] Kerr. 99.
[93] Vale. 62-63
[94] Blanchard. 6.
[95] Kerr. 107-108.
[96] *Ibid.*
[97] Kerr. 110-111.
[98] Vale. 62-63.
[99] Kerr. 108.
[100] Kerr. 109.
[101] Vale. 62.
[102] Kerr. 112-113.
[103] Kerr. 113.
[104] Kerr. 116.
[105] Grossman. 54.
[106] "Greenbrier: Five Star Fallout Shelter". CONELRAD. Retrieved 06/2006 from
http://www.conelrad.com/groundzero/greenbrier.html
[107] "Site-R Raven Rock Alternate Joint Communications Center (AJCC)
Alternate National Military Command Center". Global Security. Retrieved 06/2006 from
http://www.globalsecurity.org/wmd/facility/raven-rock.htm
[108] "Greenbrier: Five Star Fallout Shelter".
[109] *Ibid.*
[110] Blanchard. 7.
[111] "Preparing for Doomsday—Letter from President Kennedy, September 1961". *CNN.* Retrieved 06/2006 from
http://www.cnn.com/SPECIALS/cold.war/experience/the.bomb/jfk.essay/
[112] Kerr. 118.
[113] Department of the Army (1971). "Activities and Status of Civil Defense in the United States". Report by the Comptroller General. October 26, 1971. Retrieved 06/2006 from
http://archive.gao.gov/f0302/095495.pdf
[114] *Ibid.*
[115] "SEMP Biot #244: What is Civil Defense?" Suburban Emergency Management Project. Retrieved 6/2006 from
http://www.semP.us/biots/biot_244.html
[116] Kerr. 119.
[117] *Ibid.*
[118] Kerr. 120.
[119] Kerr. 121.
[120] Blanchard. 7.
[121] Blanchard. 8.
[122] Donald W. Mitchell (1966). *Civil Defense: Planning for Survival and Recovery.* (Industrial College of the Armed Forces 1966). P. 44.
[123] Mitchell. 47.
[124] SEMP Biot #244: What is Civil Defense?"
[125] *Ibid.*
[126] Kerr. 123.
[127] Kerr. 124.
[128] *Ibid.*
[129] Blanchard. 9.
[130] Kerr. 123.
[131] Kerr. 125.
[132] Kerr. 132.
[133] Kerr. 133.
[134] Robert McNamara (1967). "Mutual Deterrence". Speech in San Francisco. September 18, 1967. Retrieved 6/2006 from
http://www.atomicarchive.com/Docs/Deterrence/Deterrence.shtml
[135] Kerr. 138.
[136] Blanchard. 13.
[137] *Ibid.*

[138] *Ibid.*
[139] Kerr. 137.
[140] Ted Steinberg (2000). *Acts of God.* (Oxford University Press 2000). P. 174-175.
[141] Steinberg. 175.
[142] *Ibid.*
[143] Blanchard. 15.
[144] Kerr. 142.
[145] Kerr. 134.
[146] Kerr. 146.
[147] Blanchard. 17.
[148] "US Disaster Plans Cited as Inadequate". *The Washington Post.*
[149] Kerr. 146.
[150] John Dowling. "FEMA: Programs, Problems, and Accomplishments" in John Dowling and Evans Harnell (Eds.). *Civil Defense: A Choice of Disasters.* 1987, P. 37.
[151] Blanchard. 19.
[152] Steinberg. 175.
[153] Steinberg. 177.
[154] "129 - Special Message to the Congress on Federal Disaster Assistance". The American Presidency Project. Retrieved 9/2006 from http://www.presidency.ucsb.edu/ws/index.php?pid=2479
[155] William Kincade (1978). "Repeating History: The Civil Defense Debate Renewed". *International Security*, Volume 2, Number 3, winter. 1978, P. 100.
[156] Strategic Arms Limitations Treaty I. Atomic Archive. Retrieved 6/2006 from
http://www.atomicarchive.com/Treaties/Treaty8.shtml
[157] Anti-Ballistic Missile Treaty between the United States of America and the Union of Soviet Socialist Republics Treaty Text (May 26, 1972). Retrieved 6/2006 from
http://www.fas.org/nuke/control/abmt/text/abm2.htm
[158] Blanchard. 18.
[159] *Ibid.*
[160] Russell Dynes and E.L. Quarantelli. "The Role of Local Civil Defense in Disaster Planning". Report Series #16, University of Delaware Disaster Research Center, 1975. Retrieved 6/2006 from http://www.udel.edu/DRC/preliminary/rs16.pdf
[161] Kincade. 105.
[162] Paul Boyer (1984). "From Activism to Apathy: The American People and Nuclear Weapons, 1963-1980". *The Journal of American History.* Vol. 70, No. 4. March 1984. P. 830.
[163] "Federal Emergency Management and Homeland Security Organization: Historical Developments
and Legislative Options". Congressional Research Service. April 2006. Retrieved 6/2006 from
http://www.fas.org/sgp/crs/homesec/RL33369.pdf
[164] Executive Order 11725 (1973). *Federal Register.* Vol. 38, June 29, 1973, P. 17175.
Retrieved 6/2006 from http://www.archives.gov/federal-register/executive-orders/1973.html
[165] George Haddow and Jane Bullock (2003). *Introduction to Emergency Management.* 2003. P. 5.
[166] "Federal Emergency Management and Homeland Security Organization: Historical Developments".
[167] Richard Nixon (1974). "Statement About the Disaster Relief Act of 1974". May 22, 1974. Retrieved 9/2006 from http://www.presidency.ucsb.edu/ws/index.php?pid=4218
[168] Clarke, *Mission Improbable.*
[169] "Tennessee Civil Defense and Emergency Management History". Tennessee Civil Defense. Retrieved 6/2006 from
http://www.tnema.org/Archives/EMHistory/TNCDHistory5.htm
[170] Clarke, *Mission Improbable.*
[171] Kerr. 147
[172] Kincade. 109.
[173] Paul Hodge (1977). "Plans for City Evacuation in Case of Nuclear War Studied". *Washington Post.* January 20, 1977.
[174] Major Thad Wolfe (1979). "Soviet—United States Civil Defense tipping the strategic scale?" *Air University Review.* March/April 1979.
[175] Kincade. 109.

[176] James R. Schlesinger (1974). "Flexible Strategic Options and Deterrence" (Excerpts from the Press Conference of U.S. Secretary of Defense James R. Schlesinger on January 10, 1974. *Survival*. March/April 1974. P. 86-90.

[177] Kerr. 151-152.

[178] *Ibid.*

[179] "The Hanford Site: Historic District". US Department of Energy. June 2002. Retrieved 6/2006 from http://www.hanford.gov/doe/history/docs/rl-97-1047/Chp1.pdf

[180] Kerr. 152.

[181] Blanchard. 20.

[182] David Winsock (1977). "No Title". *The Associated Press*. October 8, 1977.

[183] Kerr. 147.

[184] Hodge. "Plans for City Evacuation".

[185] Kerr. 148.

[186] *Ibid.*

[187] Kincade. 108.

[188] Kincade. 114.

[189] Wolfe. "Soviet—United States Civil Defense".

[190] William Lanouette (1978). "The Best Civil Defense may be the Best – or Worst – Offense". *The National Journal*. September 9, 1978. Retrieved 6/2006 from http://www.jimmycarterlibrary.org/documents/prmemorandums/prm32.pdf

[191] *Ibid.*

[192] Blanchard. 21.

[193] William Lanouette (1978). "Waiting for a Signal". *The National Journal*. November 11, 1978.

[194] Tom Raum (1979). "Washington Dateline". *Associated Press*. May 16, 1979.

[195] Haddow. 5.

[196] Haddow. 5.

[197] Kerr. 159.

[198] Blanchard. 21.

[199] William Odom. "The Origins and Design of Presidential Decision-59: A Memoir" in Henry Sokolski (Ed.). *Getting MAD: Nuclear Mutual Assured Destruction, Its Origin and Practice*. Strategic Studies Institute. November, 2004. P. 178. Retrieved 6/2006 from http://www.strategicstudiesinstitute.army.mil/pdffiles/PUB585.pdf

[200] Clarke, *Mission Improbable*.

[201] Kerr. 161.

[202] Kerr. 160.

[203] Kerr. 165.

[204] Lanouette. "The Best Civil Defense".

[205] Reginald Stuart (1982). "Some Local Officials Refuse to Plan Mass Relocation in an Atom Threat". *New York Times*. May 12, 1982.

[206] Blanchard. 22.

[207] Louis Giufrrida (1984). "We Are Better Prepared for Tomorrow's Disasters: Interview with Director of FEMA". *U.S. News & World Report*. March 19, 1984.

[208] Blanchard. 22.

[209] Dowling. 38.

[210] Blanchard. 22.

[211] Vale. 78.

[212] "FEMA Plan for Revitalizing Civil Defense". GAO 8.

[213] "FEMA Plan for Revitalizing Civil Defense". GAO 1.

[214] Kerr. 166.

[215] "FEMA Plan for Revitalizing Civil Defense". GAO 6.

[216] Vale. 78.

[217] Blanchard. 23.

[218] *Ibid.*

[219] "History of Federal Disaster Mitigation: Evolution of FEMA". *Congressional Digest*. November 2005.

[220] John Lewis Gaddis (2002). *Strategies of Containment: A Critical Appraisal of American National Security Policy During the Cold War*. 2005. P. 352.

[221] John Dowling and Evans M Harrell (1987). *Civil Defense: A Choice of Disasters* (1987). P. 86.

[222] Richard Sylves and William Cumming (2004). "FEMA's Path to Homeland Security: 1979-2003". *Journal of Homeland Security and Emergency Management*. 2004.

[223] Claire B Rubin et al (2003). "Major Terrorism Events and Their U.S. Outcomes (1988-2001)." Natural Hazards Research Working Paper #107. Natural Hazards Research and Applications Information Center, University of Colorado, (March 2003). Retrieved 6/2006.

[224] *Ibid.*

[225] R. Steven Daniels. "Transforming Government: The Renewal and Revitalization of the Federal Emergency Management Agency". (Birmingham: U of Alabama, 2000). P. 12.

[226] B. Henry Hogue and Keith Bea (2006). "Federal Emergency Management and Homeland Security Organization: Historical Developments and Legislative Options." Washington, D.C.: United States Congressional Research Service, (April 19, 2006). P. 15.

[227] Daniels. 12.

[228] "Disaster Management: Recent Disasters Demonstrate the Need to Improve the Nation's Response Strategy." United States General Accounting Office. May 25, 1993. P. 3; "Disaster Assistance: Federal, State, and Local Responses to Natural Disasters Need Improvement." United States General Accounting Office. March 1991. P. 22.

[229] *Ibid.*

[230] National Security Directive 66. "Civil Defense." The White House: Washington. March 16, 1992.

[231] "Hearing on National Defense Authorization Act for Fiscal Year 1993 – H.R. 5006: Military Installations and Facilities Subcommittee Hearing on Civil Defense." Committee on Armed Services House of Representatives, 102nd Congress. Washington, D.C.: United States Printing Office. May 6, 1992. P. 3.

[232] B. Henry Hogue and Keith Bea (2006). "Federal Emergency Management and Homeland Security Organization". P. 15.

[233] National Academy of Public Administration Panel (1993). "Coping with Catastrophe: Building an Emergency Management System to Meet People's Needs in Natural and Manmade Disasters", (February, 1993). P. 1.

[234] Hogue and Bea. "Federal Emergency Management".

[235] National Academy of Public Administration Panel. P. IX.

[236] Daniels. P. 13.

[237] Hogue and Bea. 18.

[238] Sylves and Cummings. 6.

[239] Patrick S Roberts (2004). "Reputation and Federal Emergency Preparedness Agencies, 1948-2003." American Political Science Association, Annual Meeting. September 2004. P. 18.

[240] *Ibid* 19.

[241] Claire B. Rubin et al. "Major Terrorism Events and Their U.S. Outcomes (1988-2001)." *Natural Hazards Research Working Paper #107*. Natural Hazards Research and Applications Information Center, University of Colorado. Appendix A.

[242] Roberts. 19.

[243] *Ibid.* 19.

[244] Rubin. *Natural Hazards Research Working Paper #107*.

[245] "Remarks by Hon. John M. Spratt, Jr., House of Representatives, Regarding Defense Against Weapons of Mass Destruction Act of 1996." United States Congressional Record. June 17, 1996

[246] Eric P Larson and John E Peters (2001). "Preparing the U.S. Army for Homeland Security: Concepts, Issues, and Options." RAND. 2001. P. 13.

[247] Rubin. *Natural Hazards Research Working Paper #107*.

[248] *Ibid.* Appendix A.

[249] Larson and Peters. 15.

[250] *Ibid.*

[251] "Department of Defense Plan for Integrating National Guard and Reserve Component Support for Response to Attacks Using Weapons of Mass Destruction". United States Department of Defense. United States General Accounting Office (January 1998). Retrieved 6/2006 from http://www.defenselink.mil/pubs/wmdresponse/

[252] "Combating Terrorism".

[253] Presidential Decision Directive 63: Critical Infrastructure Protection, May 22, 1998.

[254] Hogue and Bea. 18.

[255] *Ibid.* 19.

[256] RAND National Security Research Division. "Gilmore Commission". Retrieved 8/2006 from http://www.rand.org/nsrd/terrpanel/

[257] Wikipedia. "Gilmore Commission". Retrieved 8/2006 from http://en.wikipedia.org/wiki/Gilmore_Commission

[258] Congressional Research Service. "9/11 Commission Recommendations: New Structures and Organizations." Retrieved from http://www.mipt.org/pdf/CRS_RL32501.pdf

[259] Tom Lansford. "Homeland Security from Clinton to Bush: An Assessment". Retrieved 6/2006 from http://www.findarticles.com/p/articles/mil m0KVD/is 4 3/ai n6142014

[260] *Ibid.*

[261] Executive Order Establishing Office of Homeland Security. White House. October 8, 2001.

[262] "Threats & Protection: Homeland Security Advisory System." United States Department of Homeland Security. Retrieved 9/2006 from http://www.dhs.gov/dhspublic/display?theme=29

[263] *Ibid.*

[264] National Strategy for Homeland Security, The White House Office of Homeland Security, July 2002, p. viii.

[265] Ibid. p. 5.

[266] "Assessing the Department of Homeland Security". Brookings Institution. July 2002.

[267] "About Ready." Ready.gov. Retrieved 9/2006 from http://www.ready.gov/america/about/

[268] "Secretary Tom Ridge on the One-Year Anniversary of the Department of Homeland Security." United States Department of Homeland Security. February 23, 2004.

[269] *Ibid.*

[270] Homeland Security Presidential Directive/Hspd-8. December 17, 2003.

[271] *Ibid.*

[272] "Department of Homeland Security Reorganization: The 2SR Initiative." Congressional Research Service. Harold C. Relyea & Henry B. Hogue. August 19, 2005.

[273] "Just the Facts, Survey by the US Conference of Mayors." United States Department of Homeland Security. July 26, 2006.

[274] *Ibid.*

[275] "Select Homeland Security Accomplishments for 2005." United States Department of Homeland Security. December 20, 2005.

[276] *Ibid.*